CW00431723

WALKS AROUND WHARFEDALE

TEN GREAT WALKS UNDER SIX MILES

Sheila Bowker

Dalesman

First published in 2012 by Dalesman
an imprint of
Country Publications Ltd
The Water Mill
Broughton Hall
Skipton
North Yorkshire BD23 3AG
www.dalesman.co.uk

Text © Sheila Bowker 2012
Maps © Gelder Design & Mapping 2012
Illustrations © Christine Isherwood 2012

Cover: Burnsall by Steve Lord

ISBN 978-1-85568-304-4

Printed in China by Latitude Press Ltd.

PUBLISHER'S NOTE
....
The information given in this book has been provided in good faith and is intended only as a general guide. Whilst all reasonable efforts have been made to ensure that details were correct at the time of publication, the author and Country Publications Ltd cannot accept any responsibility for inaccuracies. It is the responsibility of individuals undertaking outdoor activities to approach the activity with caution and, especially if inexperienced, to do so under appropriate supervision. The activity described in this book is strenuous and individuals should ensure that they are suitably fit before embarking upon it. They should carry the appropriate equipment and maps, be properly clothed and have adequate footwear. They should also take note of weather conditions and forecasts, and leave notice of their intended route and estimated time of return.

Contents

Introduction 4

Walk 1   The head of Wharfedale 5

Walk 2   Kettlewell to Starbotton 8

Walk 3   Bordley and Threshfield Moor 10

walk 4   Around and about Grassington 13

Walk 5   The Strid and Barden Tower 15

Walk 6   The Valley of Desolation 18

Walk 7   Addingham and Langbar Moor 21

Walk 8   Lindley Wood Reservoir 24

Walk 9   Ilkley Moor 27

Walk 10 Otley Chevin 30

Introduction

Beckermonds is a Norse word meaning 'meeting of the becks' and what an appropriate name, for, just north of Beckermonds in Langstrothdale, Oughtershaw Beck and Greenfield Beck merge, and the River Wharfe is born. The Wharfe then makes its long journey through the south-eastern region of the Yorkshire Dales National Park. En route, the landscape is stunningly beautiful, as Wharfedale is a region of tree-lined valleys and sheep-filled pastures topped with limestone outcrops and high fells.

Besides Man's influence on the landscape, two causes of major adjustment and alteration have happened over the millennia. The first was the creation of the North Craven Fault about 250 million years ago; evidence of the faultline can be seen towards the end of Walk 3 at Higher Heights Holes, and near the start of Walk 4 at Linton Falls. The next alteration was caused by the Ice Age, when glacial ice grooved out the land into the iconic U-shaped valley of upper Wharfedale; this is seen best on Walks 1 and 2.

Wharfedale has many stunning manmade and natural features: the rushing waters of Linton Falls; the overhanging cliff at Kilnsey Crag; the romantic ruins of Bolton Abbey; the rock formations on Ilkley Moor and Otley Chevin; attractive villages such as Buckden, Burnsall and Grassington to the north; and the smart towns of Ilkley and Otley to the south.

As far back as 1890, Rev Bailey J Harker from Grassington wrote a new kind of guide about Wharfedale which he called *The Buxton of Yorkshire, being a Complete Guide for Tourists to Grassington and Upper Wharfedale*. So I'm well aware that there's nothing new about devising and describing walks for Wharfedale, whether short or long. The region offers hundreds of miles of great walks, and I sincerely hope you enjoy the ones I have selected for you here.

Some routes have steep sections, and may be muddy underfoot after rain, so boots are advisable. Rainwear, plus emergency food and drink, should always be carried. Take a good map and compass, and know how to use them. Recommended are the OS Explorer maps 2, 30 and 297, as specified for each walk. Take all litter home with you, close gates (unless clearly propped open), keep dogs on leads at all times, and keep to public paths. For details of public transport, visit www.dalesbus.org or www.wymetro.com.

The head of Wharfedale

Distance: 5 miles (8 km). Time: 2½–3 hours.
Start/parking: Bucken, national park car park; grid ref 942773
Terrain: footpaths, bridleways and lanes. Height gained: 880 feet (270 m).
Public transport: buses to Buckden from Skipton.
Refreshments/facilities: toilets in Buckden; pubs in Cray and Hubberholme.
Map: OS Explorer OL2 – Yorkshire Dales Southern and Western.

With clear paths, super views and historical interest, this walk around the head of Wharfedale is a classic.

Take the gently rising stony track heading north from the car park, signposted for Buckden Pike and Cray High Bridge.

This is a section of the Roman road from Ilkley to Bainbridge in Wensleydale.

As the trees of Rakes Wood are cleared, a wall comes in on the left. The track bears right and levels out along Buckden Rake.

Good views come in of Langstrothdale down to the left. The River Wharfe flows shallow down pretty Langstrothdale, regularly revealing its bed of worn limestone. One of the loveliest sections of the Dales Way long-distance footpath runs along the length of the dale on its leg from Buckden to Dent.

Soon after, leave the main track as it heads up Buckden Pike. Keep straight ahead, close to the wall, and on through a gate signposted 'Cray High Bridge'.

At 2300 feet (702 m), Buckden Pike is one of the highest fells in this area, and dominates the view up ahead right.

Stay on the level grassy track as it passes through another gate and into National Trust land. Take a footpath on the left heading downhill, signposted Cray. (You can see the tiny hamlet below as you make the steep descent down the rocky hillside.) At the bottom, cross Cray Gill via the stepping stones and walk out to the lane. Cross straight over and take the track to the right-hand side of the White Lion Inn, signposted 'Stubbing Bridge 1 mile' and 'Yockenthwaite 4 miles'.

Almost immediately, the track splits. Take the right-hand option, confirmed by a footpath sign. Keep on up to the right of a barn and through a farm gate straight ahead, keeping all of the farm buildings to your left. Ford a small beck. Go straight ahead at a three-way footpath sign, staying on the obvious path and through a gate signposted 'Scar House and Yockenthwaite'.

This is one of the finest paths in Wharfedale, taking you on a limestone ledge along the contours and offering superb views to the left down-dale, with the greenery of Hay Close above, and Todd's Wood and Hubberholme Wood below, framing the picture-perfect scene.

In summer, watch out for the spotted flycatcher as it hunts for insects.

6

Pass to the left of a barn and through a gate. Then immediately, keep tight round a wall on the right and follow two footpath signs as the path swings and descends to cross the footbridge over Crook Gill. Keeping close to the fence above Todd's Wood for a while, watch out for a division of paths to turn sharp left, signposted 'Hubberholme'.

As you descend, the roofs of Scar House come into view down on the left. Scar House was rebuilt in 1876, replacing the original property built approximately 250 years earlier. George Fox reputedly visited the house in 1652 when extolling the benefits of Quakerism to the people of north-west England.

Take the obvious path round the property to join its concrete driveway as it makes its steepish descent down to Hubberholme, where the first building you'll see is the Church of St Michael & All Angels.

Dating mainly from the twelfth century and built originally as a forest chapel, Hubberholme Church sits idyllically in its riverside location. The oak pews were carved in the 1930s by Robert 'Mouseman' Thompson, so his mouse signatures are secreted around the woodwork. The ashes of the Bradford-born author J B Priestley are buried in the churchyard.

Greater bellflower grows in open woodland, its bright blue flowers appearing on tall stems in high summer.

The route joins the Dales Way coming along the river from the right, and goes through a farm gate before keeping close to the church wall as it heads towards the George Inn. Walk over the bridge spanning the Wharfe and turn left in front of the pub along Dubb's Lane. Approximately 400 yards after passing Grange Farm, stay with the Dales Way as it bears left through a wide gate almost facing the lane, signposted 'Buckden'.

Relish the pleasant riverside walk, which leads you out on to a lane just short of Buckden. Turn left over the bridge and back to the car park.

Kettlewell to Starbotton

Distance: 4¾ miles (7.5 km). **Time:** 2½ hours.
Start and parking: Kettlewell, national park car park; grid ref 967722.
Terrain: footpaths, bridleways and lanes. **Height gained:** 1,100 feet (335 m).
Public transport: buses from Skipton.
Refreshments/facilities: toilets and refreshments in Kettlewell; pub in Starbotton.
Map: OS Explorer OL2 – Yorkshire Dales Southern and Western.

This classic walk linking two of Wharfedale's loveliest villages displays the distinctive glacial U-shaping of the valley magnificently. The return walk takes you higher up the western side of the dale, with the reward of a superb panorama making it so worthwhile.

Kettlewell was granted its market charter in the thirteenth century, and the abbeys of Bolton, Fountains and Coverham all owned land close by. The lead mining and textile industries both brought development and prosperity to the village, whilst today Kettlewell is probably best known for its annual Scarecrow Festival.

From the car park, turn left into Kettlewell. Cross a bridge and take the second lane on the right, between the Blue Bell and Penny Croft B&B. When the lane swings right and widens just past Cam Lodge, keep ahead on the stony track rising up, signposted 'Starbotton 1¼ miles'. The route becomes a footpath as it veers left around the wall, then undulates gently along the eastern side of the dale, keeping parallel to the river and lane down on the left, and crossing numerous stiles and becks along the way; but nothing too difficult, so enjoy the great views along the dale.

The obvious path proceeds through woodlands and the conservation area at Cross Wood, before heading over open meadows with limestone scars up to the right. Starbotton comes into view ahead. The path turns left just before a barn and descends across fields, confirmed by a yellow marker-post and down steps with a handrail. Veer right over the next field and through a gate halfway down. Cross a narrow field to come out on the lane. (Here, the footpath sign pointing back to Kettlewell says 2 miles, yet it was only 1¾ miles the way we've come.)

The word Starbotton comes from the Old Norse word 'stannerbotton', the valley where the stakes are cut.

Turn left down to the B6160 road and cross over to take the stony, walled bridleway signposted to Arncliffe, Buckden and Kettlewell. Stay on this track down to the river. Cross the footbridge leading to a paved area and a 4-way footpath sign. Go straight ahead, signposted 'Arncliffe', and walk up an avenue of trees. Bear left round a roofless barn on an old walled path that gains altitude through shrubby terrain. The path levels slightly, then ascends again through woodland. Above Wibbertons Fields, the going is

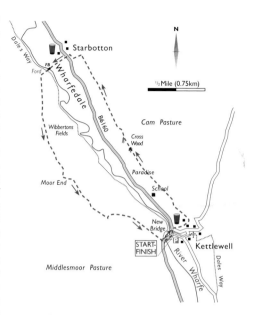

rather steep and rocky with the land on the left falling away quite steeply, but becomes a level, grassy path as you clear the trees.

This stretch provides great picnic spots with fabulous views down to the meandering river below, Starbotton to the left and Kettlewell right.

Continue along through a gate to a 3-way sign. Bear left on the bridleway. Head up to another gate, where there is a second 3-way sign; this time keep ahead, signposted 'Kettlewell'.

The path levels somewhat as it crosses a field with a wall just down on the left. Go through a gate beside a footpath sign. Keep up (ignoring sheep tracks dropping down) towards the top of the buildings at Moor End, confirmed by direction arrows, and on up through a gap in the wall. Turn left through a gate on the left, leading to the bridleway descending between the buildings at Moor End. Turn right and keep ahead on the distinct, rutted track, with a wall to the left.

The track becomes stony as it swings down the contours and is quite steep for a while, but levels before it meets the road, where you turn left, back into Kettlewell.

Bordley and Threshfield Moor

Distance: 6 miles (9.5 km). Time: 4 hours.
Start: Take Skirethorns Lane (off the B6160 just north of Threshfield) and drive to a gate beside a cattle grid where the lane becomes unfenced and is called Malham Moor Lane; grid ref 952653.
Parking: limited road-side parking at the start of the walk.
Terrain: footpaths (some indistinct in parts), bridleways and lanes; this walk is quite challenging as it's in a remote area and crosses open moorland, so would be most enjoyed during dry weather and with clear visibility; map-reading skills are helpful. Height gained: 760 feet (230 m).
Refreshments/facilities: none available.
Public transport: none available.
Map: OS Explorer OL2 – Yorkshire Dales Southern and Western.

The journey to the start is an attractive precursor to the walk, as the approach lane is bordered by pretty cottages when it's called Skirethorns Lane, dips up and down through attractive woodland when Wood Lane, rises up through a landscape of exposed limestone when called Hard Gate, to become Malham Moor Lane where it ends on open moorland.

The bird's-eye primrose has delicate little pink flowers which appear in June and July.

Continue along Malham Moor Lane to descend through a gateway. Almost immediately, bear left on a stony bridleway signposted 'Bordley ½ mile'. The track swings up, a fence comes in on the right and the surface becomes metalled, with good views to Winterburn Reservoir and Bordley below.

Tucked well off the beaten track and fronted by duck-ponds, Bordley's two properties nestle prettily amongst farmland. But door lintels hundreds of years old are reminders of when Bordley was large enough to have the status of a township, and the name Bordley Town is sometimes still used.

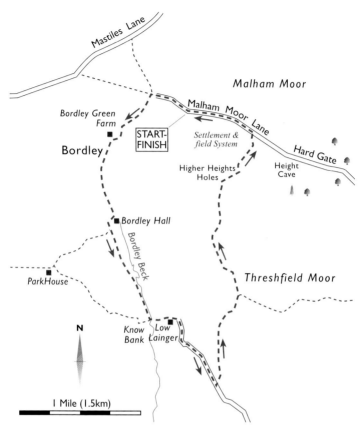

Descend down until immediately opposite Bordley Green Farmhouse. Take a narrow ginnel (passageway) along the right-hand side of a wooden-slatted barn. Bear right up a stony track, till it splits. Take the left-hand one along a rutted track, heading south through fields. Leave the track by veering slightly left where a short section of broken wall crosses, confirmed by a footpath sign. Descend to cross a stile in the bottom right-hand corner of the field. Continue ahead and through a gate in a shallow valley just to the right. Cross this field by aiming to the right of a modern barn, then keep on to bear right on a stony track, signposted 'Park House and Know Bank'.

Follow the track as it curves left and crosses a ford (two flat stone 'bridges' can be used if it's wet). At a 3-way signpost, take the left option, signposted 'Know Bank ¾ mile', by leaving the track to keep ahead, with a beck just

11

beyond a wall on the left and the land rising up to the right. The ground is rutted and the path indistinct. Keep along just above the wall until a tiny beck comes in on the right and a stile is immediately followed by a ford over a beck.

Continue in the same direction beneath overhead wires on a narrow path with Bordley Beck down left. Keep just right of a fenced copse. Descend slightly, go through a gate, then on ahead with the beck still on the left. Exit the field by turning right by a footpath sign to meet the lane. Turn left.

Follow the lane uphill, with the beck gurgling down on the left, passing the property named Low Lainger on the right. At the T-junction, where there's a phone box in front of Lainger House, bear right on a lane which ascends steeply. At an old quarry on the left

The stoat is orange-brown above and white below, with a distinctive black tip to its tail.

just prior to where the lane begins its descent, turn left on the sandy track, signposted 'Moor Lane and Threshfield 2 miles'. The track divides almost immediately. Take the left-hand option, which soon becomes rutted and grassy as it crosses Threshfield Moor, with good views of the fells on the far side of Wharfedale.

Turn left soon after a wall has come in on the left, following a bridleway sign to Malham Moor Lane. The path is narrower and sandy as it fords a beck, then swings left again and becomes a walled track, again signposted 'Malham Moor Lane'.

Where the walled track ends, a gate marked with a bridleway sign leads back on to open moorland. The route bears left, confirmed by occasional blue-topped marker posts. The track descends as a wall comes in on the left, then through two gates in quick succession on to a wide, walled path.

Here, at Higher Heights Holes, the sudden change in the landscape is due to the North Craven Fault which runs east-west across here.

At a crossing of four routes keep ahead, signposted 'Kilnsey'. Blue-topped posts guide you along a grassy sward before exiting on Malham Moor Lane, where you turn left back to the start.

Around and about Grassington

Distance: 2½ miles (4 km). Time: 1½ hours.
Start/parking: Grassington, national park car park off the Pateley Bridge
road (B6265); grid ref 004637.
Terrain: footpaths, bridleways and quiet lanes. Height gained: 250 feet (75 m).
Public transport: regular bus services to Grassington.
Refreshments/facilities: toilets at car park; refreshments in Grassington.
Map: OS Explorer OL2 – Yorkshire Dales Southern and Western.

An attractive small town with a bustling atmosphere and interesting buildings, Grassington is something of a honey-pot as the main centre for upper Wharfedale and even, some would say, the capital of the Dales.

Leave the car park at the far left-hand corner (furthest from the road) and turn right on narrow Sedber Lane, signposted 'Linton Falls'.

Linton Falls are caused by the line of the North Craven Fault crossing the River Wharfe and creating quite a spectalcle downstream from the bridge, especially when the river is in spate.

The lane descends gently so makes an attractive approach to the River Wharfe. Do wander on to the bridge to see the waterfall, but come back to the end of the lane, then, with your back to the bridge and facing up towards the car park, turn left.

Follow the obvious path, with the river on your left initially. Cut across the field, over a footbridge and up the side of the many-arched road bridge. Cross straight over the road. Take the track ahead signposted 'Wood Lane via Low Grass Wood'. Descend slightly, with a wall on the right and a fence on the left. Where both end, follow the path to the riverbank. Turn right to walk with the river on your left, enjoying nice views up to Grass Wood ahead. The path progresses through a gate and over a footbridge before it reaches Ghaistrill's Strid. (Shortly after the footbridge, observe a grassy path heading back sharp right, as this is your return route.)

The River Wharfe has two areas where its usual nonchalent flow is seriously disturbed: the Strid near Bolton Abbey and here at Ghaistrill's Strid. In both instances, the river narrows between rocks so close that it writhes with fury as it squeezes through, so please enjoy the spectacle from a safe distance.

13

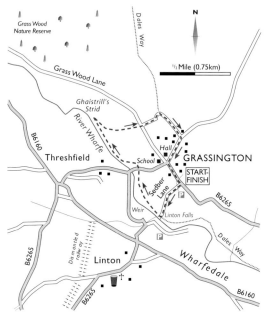

Turn back after you've enjoyed seeing Ghaisatrill's Strid, retrace your steps to the grassy path you passed earlier, and turn left. Aim for the junction of a wall and a fence, admiring the embryonic pond created by a spring, before bearing right on the path heading for the corner of a wall that comes in on the left. Keep on in the same direction and through an opening in a wall on the right. Now veer slightly left to a gateway just visible at the far left of the field, equidistant between a white building on the right and the gable end of a barn to the left.

The gateway gives access to a short, walled track leading to a metalled lane. Turn right and almost immediately left on to another narrow walled lane that ascends gently to a crossroads. Here, a bench begs to be used to savour the pastoral scene.

Go straight over on a lane that continues to ascend. Soon you're amongst Grassington's outlying properties. Turn right at a farm entrance and continue along the lane between cottages as the Dales Way route joins from the left. Grassington Methodist Church with its charming rural-scened murals is passed on the left. At another crossroads, turn right down the main street with its quaint shops and pretty cobbled market place on the left. At the T-junction with the main B6265 road, turn left back to the car park.

14

The Strid and Barden Tower

Distance: 4 miles (6.5 km). Time: 2 hours.
Start/parking: car park just north of Barden Bridge on the Barden to
Appletreewick road; grid ref GR 053574.
Terrain: footpaths and bridleways; no stiles. Height gained: 570 feet (175 m).
Public transport: buses to Bolton Abbey Estate.
Refreshments/facilities: at Cavendish Pavilion
Map: OS Explorer OL2 – Yorkshire Dales Southern and Western,
or OS Explorer 297 – Lower Wharfedale & Washburn Valley.

Looking at the map, this route might appear boring: along one side of the river and back on the other but it's a lovely walk and, as the Bolton Abbey Estate is such an icon of Wharfedale, not to visit would be an injustice.

Walk from the car park towards Barden Bridge, but don't cross. Instead, keep straight ahead through a gate leading to the Bolton Abbey Estate.

The earlier bridge spanning the Wharfe at Barden was destroyed in the flood of 1673 and the current one, with its three graceful arches, was constructed three years later.

The Bolton Abbey Estate is one of the seats of the Duke of Devonshire, but he resides at his other, even more famous, home — Chatsworth House in Derbyshire.

Follow the wide, grassy path to the riverbank. The route now keeps close to the river on your right all the way to the Wooden Bridge beside Cavendish Pavilion.

There are benches and seats dotted along where you can sit and watch the waterfowl, or enjoy the views to Barden Fell and Simon's Seat up on the left.

The path negotiates round a quite ornate bridge and past a very grand stone seat. (After this it's shown on the OS map as a red dotted line, meaning it's a permissive path.) Rise up through Strid Wood Site of Special Scientific Interest, an area of sessile oak trees and rare plants, where the undulating path occasionally has exposed rocks and tree roots. The land falls away a little steeply at times, with beautiful views down to the river, especially as the Strid is neared — you'll know when you're close from the noise.

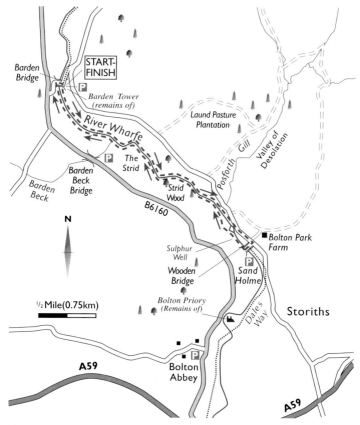

The Strid is where the River Wharfe flows furious and fast as it churns through a narrow channel of softer limestone. Up to 25 feet (8 m) deep, the channel widens towards the bottom, making the Strid potentially very dangerous — so please admire it from a distance.

The track ascends as the river flows wide and gentle again. There is a useful shelter with seats, inscribed 'Harrison's Ford Seat'. The track widens as it levels with the river and comes close to Storiths Lane, and continues ahead signposted 'Cavendish Pavilion and Bolton Abbey'. The river widens further as it negotiates the moss-covered boulders around Lud Stream Islands. The route is close to a fence on the right as the path descends down steps and through a meadow. Cross the Wooden Bridge, turn right, and Cavendish Pavilion and its facilities are all here.

The pavilion was built in memory of Lord Frederick Cavendish, son of the 7th Duke of Devonshire who, just hours after becoming Ireland's Secretary of State in 1881, was murdered in Dublin.

(If you wish to see the famous ruined priory of Bolton Abbey, follow the signposted track, but then return to this spot to continue our walk.)

The return, which is mostly on the Dales Way route, has the river on the right, and is along a wide, level track most of the way, following green-arrowed direction posts to Barden Bridge.

If you would like to experience the Sulphur Well, bear right a short distance from the pavilion (where signposted to the well), along a narrow, rocky path with exposed roots that takes you down past the well, then climbs steps to bring you back to the main track.

Monkeyflower (front) and meadowsweet (back) are found in damp areas and on river margins.

The river is very picturesque as it bends right just prior to the Strid. The path rises up and the noise of rushing water increases. Please take notice of the 'Danger' warning signs and, ideally, stay on the track as it continues up to a junction. Turn right. Where the track turns left, leave it to take the narrow path on the right. This rejoins the wide track again after a while. Where it splits, bear right downhill, following signs to Barden Bridge.

A footbridge over Barden Beck is crossed where the path exits woodland, and a fence comes in on the left with fields rising up beyond. Keep straight on past the ornate footbridge.

There are good views ahead of Barden Tower. Situated within the ancient Forest of Barden, Barden Tower was constructed in the early sixteenth century by Lord Henry Clifford as a hunting lodge, one of six built within the Forest. Barden Tower was rebuilt by Lady Anne Clifford in the mid-seventeenth century, but it is now a rather romantic ruin.

Climb the steps beside Barden Bridge up to the road. Bear right, then left, back to the car park.

Walk 6

The Valley of Desolation

Distance: 4½ miles (7 km). Time: 2½ hours.
Start/parking: Sand Holme car park, Bolton Abbey Estate; grid ref 078551.
Terrain: footpaths, bridleways, short section on quiet lane; very few stiles;
dogs not allowed on this part of the Estate. Height gained: 830 feet (255 m).
Public transport: buses to Bolton Abbey Estate.
Refreshments/facilities: at Cavendish Pavilion.
Map: OS Explorer OL2 – Yorkshire Dales Southern and Western,
or OS Explorer 297 – Lower Wharfedale & Washburn Valley.

From the car park, cross the River Wharfe by the Wooden Bridge situated just before Cavendish Pavilion. Turn immediately left along the riverbank. Head right, up the slope, signposted 'Valley of Desolation'. Turn left along Storiths Lane for a short distance. Leave it just prior to an '18% gradient' sign at the top of a brow, where you turn right through a gate in the wall.

Follow the obvious track (a permissive path), leading round a property and across parkland. Go through a kissing-gate beside a high metal gate. Continue up the stony track to a seating area and information panel explaining about the Valley of Desolation.

The Valley of Desolation is so called following considerable destruction that was caused by a violent storm in 1826. Today, the secretive valley is calm and verdant, its beauty enhanced by pretty waterfalls, and ferns growing amongst strewn boulders.

The track continues through parkland and passes a small lake before ascending to the viewpoint for Posforth Gill Falls on the left.

Posforth Gill waterfall tumbles down a height of 50 feet (15 m).

Meadow cranesbill has blueish-purple flowers.

18

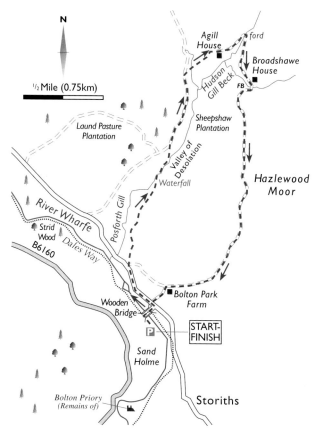

The track continues up with a fence on the left. As another track comes in from the right, bear left where there are fences on both sides. The track is soon replaced by a footpath which winds upwards, with the beck down on the left. Cross the footbridge. Continue on, with a beck now on your right. Where the path divides, take the left option. Rise diagonally up the valley side as the beck down below veers away to the right. The route goes through a gate, followed by a sign for Simon's Seat as woodland is entered, then crosses over another track to head up through fir trees.

Leave the woodland and continue over lovely heather-clad moorland for about 200 yards. Take the grassy path with a wall on the right that descends to a beck. Ford the beck and climb up the other side. Cross a step-stile on

The grey wagtail favours fast-flowing rivers and streams.

the right just past a gate. Follow the grassy path uphill which heads to the clump of trees on the skyline surrounding Agill House (which is just a barn). Cross a couple of fields to pass to the right of the building. (Some more buildings are a little way off to the right; this is Broadshawe which you will pass in a short while.)

Continue on the grassy sward. Go through a wide gate with a small gate at right-angles. Gradually descend to cross the beck via a flat concrete bridge (marked 'ford' on the map). The route is now a track which swings up and through another small gate. At Broadshawe, walk between the buildings and through a gate to join a track. Bear right down to cross the footbridge over Rom Shaw Dike. The grass-centred track swings up and is soon crossing open, panoramic moorland before descending slightly through a gate.

There are enchanting views down to Wharfedale and Bolton Priory in its riverside setting. The romantic ruins of the thirteenth-century Augustinian priory lie in a sweeping bend in the river, and have mesmerised numerous artists through the centuries, including J M W Turner.

Follow the track across farmland as the descent increases. Keep right where it splits to go through the farmyard at Bolton Park Farm. As you pass the farmhouse on your left, the track becomes a metalled lane. This descends quite steeply for a brief distance before it meets Storiths Lane. Go straight over the lane on a track which soon brings you to the Wooden Bridge. Cross the river and turn left back to the car park.

Walk 7

Addingham and Langbar Moor

Distance: 4 miles (6.5 km). Time: 2 hours.
Start: suspension bridge over the River Wharfe, off Bark Lane, just east of Addingham; grid ref 084499.
Parking: on-street parking on Bark Lane, or in and around Addingham.
Terrain: footpaths, bridleways and quiet lanes; can be muddy in places.
Height gained: 600 feet (185 m).
Refreshments/facilities: plenty of choice in Addingham.
Public transport: regular bus services.
Map: OS Explorer 297 – Lower Wharfedale & Washburn Valley.

Possibly due to its position nestling between Rombalds Moor in the south and Langbar Moor to the north-east, land around Addingham has been inhabited since the Bronze Age. Once known as Long Addingham as the village grew round three centres over a mile (1.5 km) or so apart, the village ceased being mostly a farming community when the textile trade arrived in the eighteenth and nineteenth centuries, when five mills were constructed.

Start the walk on Bark Lane, just east of the village centre. Join the Dales Way route across the suspension bridge over the River Wharfe. Keep straight ahead with a small beck on the right. After West Hall, bear left along a metalled track. Join West Hall Lane where it bends and there is a little triangle of grass in the centre. Turn right along this quiet lane.

Soon there are nice views down to the River Wharfe on the right. As the lane rises up towards Nesfield, you can see what remains of Castleberg Fort up on a bumpy hillock to the right.

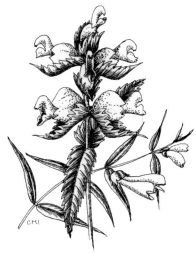

Yellow-rattle (centre) and cow-wheat (right) are found on undisturbed grassland between May and September

21

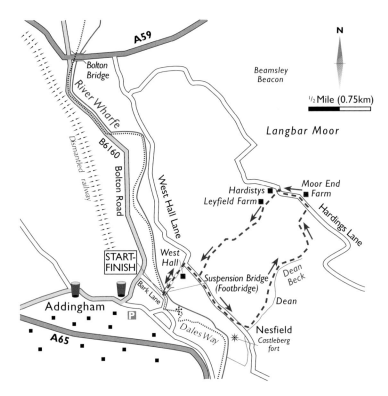

Just past the phone box, bear left up a track with a grassy centre, passing Sycamore House on the left. Keep right at the Green and descend the lane slightly. Go left through a gate along a farm track, signposted as a footpath to Dean Farm. The track ascends, with Dean Beck down on the right. Just after passing the farm and as a house comes into view ahead, bear left on a footpath marked with a faded yellow arrow on a tree. Walk up through a gate and along the grassy path through bracken straight ahead.

This is a delightful section where the path hugs the higher land as Dean Beck courses along through its secretive wooded valley to the right.

The path may be muddy and the land drops quite steeply away to the side occasionally. A wall comes in on the left. After going through a gate and striding a shallow ford, walk up to meet a metalled lane by an impressive gate on the left.

The golden plover is an archetypal bird of the Dales uplands. It is identifiable by its golden upperparts.

Bear left through a gate on a track giving access to moorland at Langbar. Bear left again on a path. Keep fairly close to the wall on the left that dog-legs a couple of times, before striking away slightly right on a path through bracken up to Hardings Lane, which is unfenced as it crosses the moor. (The path can be indistinct, so if you miss it, just past a white-painted house turn right on a rough track to Moor Croft which gives access to Hardings Lane.)

Beamsley Beacon, 1,296 feet (395 m) high and approximately three-quarters of a mile (1.2 km) north of here, is probably the best-known height on Langbar Moor. As this edge of the moor stands tall over the lower lands surrounding it to the south-west, Beamsley was one of the chain of fire beacon sites used to transmit warnings at times of emergency in the days before the telegraph was invented. The hill the Beacon stands on is more correctly called Howber Hill and, together with Langbar Moor, forms the western end of a large area of open moorland which spreads to the Washburn Valley. The moor offers fine, panoramic views across Wharfedale.

When you reach Hardings Lane, turn left. Pass Moor End Farm on the right. Leave the lane by turning left along a farm track just prior to a property called Hardistys. Turn left again into Leyfield Barn yard, following yellow direction arrows. (The route seems to have been diverted here so could pose a bit of a challenge, but basically just follow the yellow direction arrows.) Go right just beyond where a concrete-walled barn is a short distance away on the right, through a wide metal gate. Cross a fence by a step-stile. Head left down to cross another fence by a step-stile and bear right.

That's the route-finding challenge accomplished, so enjoy this section of the walk as it descends very gently along a grassy, level track through a delightful wooded valley past a fallen tree with a beck on the left.

The path crosses a wall via a step-stile into a field on the right, but keeps on basically in the same direction, with a fence and the beck on the left. Cross a step-stile beside a gate, and on down a large field and through a gate out onto West Hall Lane. Turn right to the triangle of grass, where you turn left back past West Hall and retrace your steps over the suspension bridge.

Lindley Wood Reservoir

Distance: 4½ miles (7 km). **Time:** 2½ hours.
Start/parking: Stainburn Forest Norwood Edge car park on the
B6451 Otley to Dacre road; grid ref 209509.
Terrain: footpaths, bridleways, quiet lanes and a short road section.
Height gained: 950 feet (290 m).
Public transport: none available.
Refreshments/facilities: none available.
Map: OS Explorer 297 – Lower Wharfedale & Washburn Valley.

Stainburn Forest covers 530 acres (215 ha) in the heart of the Washburn Valley, and numerous forest mountain-biking routes commence from Norwood Edge car park.

From the car park, turn right along the road. Almost immediately take a step-stile (signposted 'RA Lower Wharfedale Footpath Group') on the right at the edge of Warren Plantation. Walk down the field. As the woodland edge bears away right, the path continues in the same direction down to a step-stile leading back on to the B6451. Turn right, downhill. As the road starts to level out, reach a property on the left with a wide, stone-walled opening in front with a tree in the centre bearing a handwritten signpost to Leathley. Walk between the pair of old, pointed-topped gateposts on to a stony track through woodland for the length of the reservoir, a little way to the right.

The jay is a colourful woodland bird, with a loud 'kraah' call.

Lindley Wood is the most southerly of the Washburn Valley's four reservoirs, the others being Thruscross, Fewston and Swinsty. With a reputation as possibly the prettiest, Lindley Wood is the eldest of the four having been built in 1875, but is the baby in size measuring just 117 acres (47 ha).

The track, which deviates away from the water just once to cross a walled bridge over Greystone Beck, gradually becomes rougher and possibly muddy in places. The

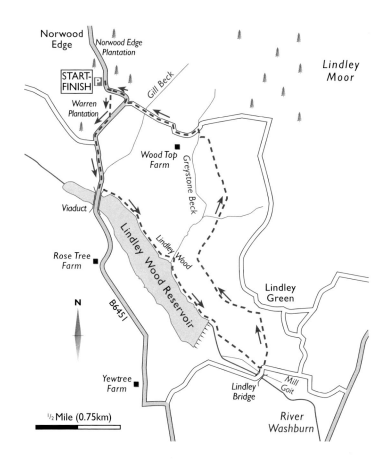

Norwood
Edge

Norwood Edge
Plantation

Lindley
Moor

START-
FINISH

Gill Beck

Warren
Plantation

Wood Top
Farm

Greystone Beck

Viaduct

Lindley Wood

Lindley Wood Reservoir

Rose Tree
Farm

N

B6451

Lindley
Green

Yewtree
Farm

Lindley
Bridge

Mill
Goit

River
Washburn

½ Mile (0.75km)

track continues ahead after the dam wall through woodlands, to exit between
another pair of pointed gateposts on to the lane by Lindley Bridge.

Turn left uphill along the lane for a few paces, before heading sharp left up
a short track and taking a footpath on the right, confirmed with yellow
arrows, along a narrow, ascending path with a wall on the right. A step-stile
leads into the bottom of a field. A grassy path heads uphill in the same
direction, keeping the wall on the right.

Bear left away from the wall before a cross-wall curves in to the right-hand
side. The gradient steepens as the path swings left then right, but straightens

again when Lindley Green Farm can be seen up ahead. Turn left just before the buildings and keep the perimeter wall on your right as you go through a gate marked with a yellow arrow.

The land on the left drops down, revealing lovely views over the Washburn Valley and Wharfedale beyond, making this a pleasant picnic spot.

This grassy path retains altitude, goes over a step-stile and comes out on to a track. Turn left, through woodland. After a cattle grid, continue along a field with a fence on the left and Lindley Wood Farm ahead. Walk just to the right of the buildings. Keep close to the boundary fence. Where the fence drops away sharply and becomes a wall, leave it by going half-right to maintain altitude along an old, levelled track.

Soon there is a broken wall on the left, and a yellow marker arrow where a wall comes in on the right. The obvious path continues between broken walls across a field, then descends through trees just beyond a gate, and crosses a tributary of Greystone Beck. Continue between broken-down walls. Pass a derelict building on the right. Keep straight ahead where another route branches off right.

Wood sage can be found alongside woodland tracks and on heathland.

After crossing a tiny beck, the path is fainter as it heads slightly left uphill. Swing right up to a stone step-stile in a short section of wall at the top right-hand corner of the field, leading into a narrow strip of land. Cross straight over and exit this narrow strip via a broken-down wall. Continue in the same direction. Keep ahead over another broken-down cross-wall, confirmed by a yellow arrow, into a reedy field.

Follow the wall as it swings left, where a marker post points the direction round to the right of gorse bushes. The route drops and rises across a couple of damp sections, and eventually meets a metalled lane. Turn left on the lane and through a wide gate.

Cross another tributary of Greystone Beck, and on past Wood Top Farm on the left. Continue on the lane as it rises up and bends right and left before becoming partially tree-lined as it leads down to cross Gill Beck and up to the road. Turn right to walk uphill back to the car park.

Ilkley Moor

Distance: 2¼ miles (3.5 km). Time: 1½ hours.
Start/parking: Darwin Gardens/Millennium Green car park, Wells Road,
Ilkley; grid ref 118471.
Terrain: footpaths, bridleways and pavement. Height gained: 670 feet (205 m).
Refreshments/facilities: toilets at White Wells car park;
refreshments at White Wells and Cow & Calf Rocks, and in town centre.
Public transport: regular buses and trains to Ilkley.
Map: OS Explorer 297 – Lower Wharfedale & Washburn Valley.

Reputed to have been written by a Sunday School party whilst visiting the area, 'On Ilkla Moor Baht 'At' – Yorkshire's 'national anthem' – has probably made Ilkley Moor the best-known stretch of moorland in England. The name, Ilkley, was derived from the Roman place-name Olicana, and a Roman fort once stood where the parish church is today.

Turn right out of the car park along the road as it gains elevation, passing the rear of Wells House on the right. Leave the road by turning left on the wide, stony track signposted 'Millennium Way'. Pass White Wells car park. The track ascends and bears left over a shallow, paved ford with narrow waterfalls trickling down to the left. Continue on up to White Wells.

It was during the Victorian era that Ilkley developed with significance and stature as a spa town famous for its hydropathic remedies, and White Wells became a popular place to 'take the waters'.

Head uphill along a stony and sandy track located behind the buildings, once again signposted 'Millennium Way'.

Sightings of buzzards in Wharfedale have become more common in recent years.

27

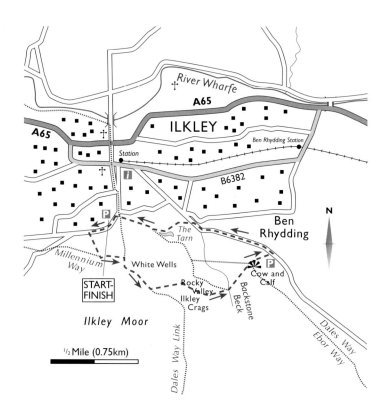

The outcrops of Ilkley Crag and West Rock can be seen up ahead.

The track ascends, to where it splits. Take the left-hand, more level option (leaving the other as it steps up a ridge). Pass below the craggy outcrop of West Rock up on the right. The route has become a narrow, rocky path as it ascends the boulder-strewn landscape through appropriately named Rocky Valley, at the end of which the path divides. Bear left, heading for the Cow & Calf Rocks (an aid to navigation is a mast which is on a hilltop immediately above them across the valley).

The Cow & Calf Rocks are a large formation consisting of a sizeable outcrop with a smaller boulder close by, like a cow with its calf. They take pride of place in their domineering position high above Ilkley and, being millstone grit, are popular with rock climbers.

The narrow path now descends and fords rock-strewn Backstone Beck, a lovely spot for a picnic. The path levels out across reedy heather moorland, with a sunken area on the left which could almost make a natural amphitheatre. Continue over a short section of grassy plateau, Suddenly you're almost on top of the Cow Rock, so take care and bear right on to the well-worn track that swings left round the rocks.

A car park and refreshment kiosk come into view below. Numerous seats are dotted around so you can sit and enjoy the view.

The wheatear has a distinctive 'chak-chak' call which sounds like two stones being knocked together.

Keep left on the paved path almost beneath the rocks. Turn right on a wider paved track, heading quite steeply downhill to the car park. Walk out to the road and cross to the pavement on the far side when safe. Turn left along the pavement as the road descends down to Ilkley.

There are pavements on both sides of the road as you proceed through a gate beside a cattle grid, so cross back over the road then, at a roundabout, turn left up a short, wide lane situated just before Craiglands Hotel. Go through a narrow gate at the right of a pair of wide gates on to a footpath. This divides almost immediately by a two-way footpath direction sign. Take the route up steps ahead. Keep on the path as it turns right and ascends through shrubby undergrowth, before it bears left and splits again. Take the right-hand choice. This soon merges with another path from the right to climb steps leading to the edge of Ilkley Tarn. Turn right along the wide metalled track, with the lake on your left.

Ilkley Tarn, popular in Victorian times for ice skating when frozen over, is very pretty with waterfowl, seats and a shelter, so makes a good place to pause and feed the ducks.

The track finishes at a wide metal gate at the end of the lake. Bear left up a grassy slope to pass to the right of the paddling pool. Continue over the grassy mound and back to the car park ahead.

Millennium Green was built in memory of Charles Darwin, who was resident in Ilkley with his family when his landmark book On The Origin of Species *was published in November 1859, and 'took the waters' at White Wells during his stay. The green has numerous features to enjoy.*

29

Otley Chevin

Distance: 4¾ miles (7.5 km). Time: 2½ hours.
Start/parking: Lower Shawfield car park, East Chevin Road, Otley;
grid ref 216443.
Terrain: footpaths, bridleways and quiet lanes. Height gained: 700 feet (215 m).
Public transport: regular buses to Otley, ½ mile (0.8 km) from start point.
Refreshments/facilities: only available in Otley.
Map: OS Explorer 297 – Lower Wharfedale & Washburn Valley.

Leave the car park at the far end, furthest from the road. Turn sharp left along the bridleway running round the car park's perimeter fence and descending through woodland. After crossing a footbridge, the path ends further along East Chevin Road. Turn left for a short distance (but observe the path going up the left-hand side of Danefield House immediately opposite, as this is the return path). Turn right over a stile signposted 'Carlton'. Follow the path uphill beside a wall on the left.

Almost immediately there are good views back over Otley and Wharfedale.

Continue in the same direction across fields. Bear left across the corner of the last one to reach York Gate lane. Cross straight over on to a track through pleasant deciduous woodland, confirmed by a footpath sign. Bear left after a few paces on to a more grassy path which may be a little boggy. A fence comes in on the left as the path becomes a wide, grassy sward. Cross a stile into a field. Continue ahead on the obvious path, firstly with a wall and then a hedge on the left.

Enjoy the fine views across the Aire Valley. South of Skipton, the River Aire flows into the wide floodplain of the Aire Valley where it meets industrialisation as it continues through Keighley, Bingley and Leeds, and ends its journey at the North Sea as part of the Humber Estuary.

Cross a stile in the left-hand corner of a fence. Follow the fence as it curves left, marked by yellow arrows. Work diagonally left across the last field on an indistinct path. Exit on to Carlton Lane opposite a junction at East Carlton. Turn right to pass Old Hall and onwards along the lane.

This stretch makes pleasant walking through rural, rolling countryside, with panoramic views to the left.

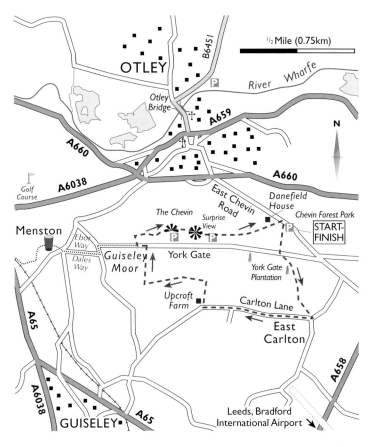

Leave the lane as it narrows, taking a bridleway on the right adjacent to Upcroft Farm and properties called Bowood and Chevin Chase. This wide, cobbled track rises up and swings left in front of Spring Field Farm.

The lane joins another track by a house called Highfield (with a wind generator in the garden). Turn right, along the edge of Guiseley Moor. The track might be muddy after rain.

Enjoy the moorland views over Wharfedale, with Menston and Burley-in-Wharfedale down to the left.

The track ends further along York Gate. Turn left for a short distance, before turning right on the path signposted 'Chevin Forest Park'.

Chevin Forest Park is a local nature reserve covering 700 acres (285 ha) of woodland and craggy escarpments, with stunning views down across the market town of Otley and lower Wharfedale beyond.

The plaintive call and bubbling song of the curlew on the moors of lower Wharfedale is a sure sign that spring has arrived.

The obvious path rises up towards the left-hand corner of woodland. Cross a stile leading into the woods. Bear right, and keep close to the wall just crossed. The path has exposed tree roots as it bears left round two huge boulders. It passes a 'Chevin Geological Trail 4' marker post, then widens as it continues in the same direction. Keep the wall on the right (it becomes a fence and is a little further away for a while before turning back into a wall). Ascend past another marker post to meet the wall at a corner, where another path joins from the right. The path dog-legs left and right before continuing in the same direction, to rise again as it leaves the woods.

There are more good views of Otley and lower Wharfedale down to the left.

Descend to the left to join another track. Keep ahead through a terrain of gorse, heather and brambles. A fence comes in up to the right as the views widen across Wharfedale. When rocks are stacked up on the right, follow the track round them up to the summit to enjoy the 360° Surprise View.

Continue the walk in the same direction. Pass a car park on your right. Keep along on the level with a wall on the right, ignoring a path dropping down left. The route exits Chevin Forest Park through a gap-stile beside a wide gate. Continue ahead down a stony track with a wall on the left. Emerge at East Chevin Road beside Danefield House. Cross the road and follow the outward route back to the car park.